Heavy Little Things

poems by

Shana Ross

Finishing Line Press
Georgetown, Kentucky

Heavy Little Things

Copyright © 2022 by Shana Ross
ISBN 978-1-64662-909-1 First Edition

All rights reserved under International and Pan-American Copyright Conventions. No part of this book may be reproduced in any manner whatsoever without written permission from the publisher, except in the case of brief quotations embodied in critical articles and reviews.

ACKNOWLEDGMENTS

Grateful acknowledgement to the following publications, in which these poems first appeared:

Anapest Journal: "Cuppa"
Anti-Heroine Chic: "Shevirah" and "Ice in the Desert"
Apeiron Review: "Spring Cleaning"
Chautauqua Journal: "How To Write A Joke"
Henniker Review: "Every Morning before the Bus"
Liminality: "Two Kinds of People"
Lion and Lilac: "Haunting"
Minor literature: "Nakedness: A Suite in Five Dances"
Poetica Review: "Irony"
Ruminate: "Blessings"
SHANTIH Journal: "Some Facts For This Moment"
Street Light Press: "Raccoon Attack"
The Hellebore: "My Grief Has Not Faded She Has Split Herself In Two"
The Westchester Review: "Whose Side Are You On" and "Here For It All"

Publisher: Leah Huete de Maines
Editor: Christen Kincaid
Cover Art: Florian Pircher, Pixaby
Author Photo: Shana Ross
Cover Design: Elizabeth Maines McCleavy

Order online: www.finishinglinepress.com
also available on amazon.com

Author inquiries and mail orders:
Finishing Line Press
PO Box 1626
Georgetown, Kentucky 40324
USA

Table of Contents

Cuppa 1

Nakedness I 2

Two Kinds of People 3

Shevirah 4

Nakedness II 6

Every Morning before the Bus 7

Blessings 8

How to Write a Joke 10

Ice in The Desert 12

Nakedness III 14

Spring Cleaning 15

Raccoon Attack 18

Americana 19

Revelation, In One Act 21

Finalists In the One Word Play Contest 22

With A Heavy Heart I Must Tell You 23

Nakedness IV 24

Some Facts for This Moment 25

My Grief Has Not Faded, She Has Split Herself In Two 26

Whose Side Are You On 27

Nakedness V 28

Irony 29

Haunting 30

The Sun Is Just Another Every Day Grief 31

Here for It All 32

Thanks 33

Cuppa

My son grins and says the microwave only shows hours and minutes when it's being a clock but does seconds when it's cooking so when it appears to be a clock I know it's still counting them, it just keeps them in its head until it's time to tell us. Now is a new minute. Inside, outside, it all makes sense. I am not sure about the counting but I am sure that everything has personality if not a soul, whatever that is, and I will be OK with the singularity for that reason. I reach in for the boiling water to make the tea and a pool gathers next to the mug, impossible to tell yet whether the flaw is in my pour and haste or a crack in the ceramic giving way in this moment. Now, why not now? Everything crumbles on its own schedule, not yours.

Nakedness I

The parents are in the kitchen opening wine and putting dinner into bowls to take to the table, weekly ritual of ending the week, beginning to breathe, continuing conversations. It is what happy people might recognize as family. Suddenly they are all aware at the same moment of screams from outside where the children are playing, intense and bloodcurdling, the serious kind of screams and everyone rushes to the door, certain that someone is destined for the ER tonight, stomachs flipping as they plummet. Silent and instantaneous prayers are flung into the universe, one mom registers the discomfort of a zero sum game in her whisper: please not my child, please not my child.

Two Kinds of People

Here's another duality: there are those who learn
time travel is possible, and instantly realize the sanctity of loss,
however overbearing the grief
that has ripped at hidden flesh and still gnaws,

rat king curled in your throat. These deaths, inextricable
from our lives, which have grown on,
however twisted and scarred. The absence of
your loved ones will be subsumed

in the sudden possibility, the pain
releases like an orgasm and acceptance is total
in the moment we reject the undoing.
And then there's the other kind of people,

those who would stop at nothing to bring their loved ones back.
The silence means you are asking yourself, now.

Shevirah

You say break and people think of vessels
fragile things holding something else
there is the shatter, the spill, the fragments and ruined insides

everything sharp and disconnected from what was
I think of breaking like waves.
I have a theory that waves are as singular as snowflakes,

energy embodied for miles, then at the end of one story
reabsorbed and returned to the sea for what's next.
The concept of infinity sinks into you and you see

science requires faith, even when the observation is complete.
Moving parts, magic lanterns
that which is full of light

that which exists only through contrast
we are stuck in moments that whir past
embrace the illusion that a story unfolds

in the repeating circle.
turn light over in your hand and
from this angle we might call it hope.

Darkness breaks into fear, despair
is it the absence of light or is light the absence of darkness or
are they unrelated companions that travel together and

do not interfere with each other's nature?
It's exhausting, thinking like you
normal people think—I am full of fear

full of hope, breaking constantly on the rocks
and the energy has to go somewhere.
It's razor sharp, the boundary between

I got this and Oh fuck
I'm drowning please
help me no run away I'm beyond

saving—no daylight between
where I bounce back and forth
trying to balance and my feet

bleed where the fine line cuts through.
I no longer believe in opposites
everything nestles more like bodies pressed

so close they overlap like atom clouds
you could say they are still one and one but
they are a new thing full of each other.

I am always full of joy and despair, brokenness and return
but only see one at a time
shuttling between, shaking shivering shattering

in the reconciliation of my truths.
Dear god, make me a zoetrope
where the light and the dark and the glimpses between

blur into more, into meaning, into motion
faster and faster until you refocus and see
horses racing, someone dancing.

Nakedness II

In the yard between two trees a slack line stretches over soft grass, border with mulch. Rings and rope hang from it. Everyone loves to test their strength on this ninja line. The children take turns fairly. One announces she will perform naked and takes off her clothes. Here is her full self, in the moment, in the air. And the other children say NO, you can't, but they are already wrong about that, so they say no, you aren't supposed to, and they say I'm telling. And the boy is scared because he knows he is not supposed to see private parts and he is scared that he will get in big trouble for this even though he hasn't done anything wrong and he panics and yells for his parents but since he doesn't know how to describe any of this, it comes out in a scream with no words. The naked girl hears the scream and realizes she has made a mistake and screams because she cannot prevent whatever will happen next, not now, there's no going back, but she blocks the boy from the door to the house on instinct, to delay the inevitable reckoning, and he screams louder now because he can't get to his mommy without going through her and in overload, he can't see what happens next and so it feels like an uncertain state where he could be trapped forever between cause and effect and it is still not his fault but everything is wrong and his screams get louder yet. And the older sister screams now too, because no one wants to be left out.

Every Morning Before The Bus

He started out measuring the driveway in feet
sneakers stacking heel to toe to heel to toe and
unsteady like a tightrope on the black pavement
he unwinds himself and stretches to claim
a place in the understanding of the world.

But at the end of there and back he could not stop so now
he counts footsteps like neverending rosary
he has never been to five hundred before
without skipping a single step
it's possible there is no such thing as math
that is truly abstract or theoretical until you are grown
and wonder fades.

Breathe in, breathe out, keep walking
the smallness of this territory
is what makes it whole, holy.

Blessings
after Erika Meitner, for JW

Bless this distress, my life hitting existential turbulence. Independently, the world seems to be going to hell. But I have awoken this morning.

Bless my certainty that I will not be able to keep up appearances today. Bless the decision, which barely surfaces to my consciousness, to go to the park. Bless the autopilot that drives me, and bless the idea that is a word that is SEEK that is seared into my brain, even though I am not sure what I'm looking for.

Bless the sour breath I take as I step out of the car in the parking lot, flavored by the tension in my shoulders, the steel cage made from my own flesh that keeps me upright, a pain I ignore like a shark ignores the constant motion of survival.

Bless my ability to tell the difference between this breath and the one before.

Bless the decision to be here, to choose a walk in the woods, to flail instead of sinking, to try anything new, to follow through and take my body to carry out my intentions.

Bless the infinite ways humans can interact with the world's beauty.

Bless my first breath on the trail, of honeysuckle, familiar sweetness, plentiful.

Bless the second band of fragrance on the breeze, the wild roses that grown by the stream, and the pause in my steps on the footbridge, even though I have barely started to walk. Are these really roses? What do I know about roses and wild roses? I ask the small stream that tumbles so fast its motion that cannot be captured on my iphone, guaranteeing it cannot be killed and pinned to a page as proof of existence.

Bless the losing of my train of thought in the running water.

Bless the meadow to my right as the trail veers to the left and heads into the forest.

Bless the blurred lines between grass and hay, the scent overlapping like bodies in a pas de deux.

Bless the dogshit that comes next.

Bless the woods, the spice of pine, the velvet decay of damp dirt, the dappling of everything as unfelt breeze flies above and rustle of one animal and then next. Bless the crawling of my skin as it remembers this place.

Bless my neighbors who walk faster or started sooner and make my increasing liberation not solitude.

Bless the gigantic black spider who crosses my path and bless my foot that alters its course and does not meet it and bless my lack of curiosity that does not stop me in my tracks for a closer look.

Bless my looping path that brings me back, at the end, to repeat: dogshit, hay, roses, honeysuckle.

Bless the car keys I have not lost.

Bless my fear and hesitation to leave, to leave so soon, to return.

You shall take in.
You shall be satisfied.
And you shall bless.

I know blessing and prayer and words and ritual and body and grace and anguish and contentment and supplication. I suspect they are not one thing, but as I travel through them I cannot find their edges, and they mix on my tongue in new blends with every breath.

How To Write A Joke

1. Setup, punch.

I'll love you forever
I say to my kid,
meaning it.

You mean until you die,
he counters.

On the train we sped by ruins
factories and warehouses in the process of
being reclaimed by nature and/or squatters.

I think they are halfway between sad and beautiful
I said to fill the silence.
And a little scary, he said, untroubled.
Like you.

2. Rule of three (and other lists)

My son has gone to school and written a list.
Likes: turtles, cats, medium salsa, taekwondo, werewolves, dogs.
Dislikes: anchovies, mushrooms,
        reading, kissing,
           love.

I would be more upset but
I know the dog thing is a bold-faced lie, plus
he eats anchovies with gusto.
His credibility is strained from the start.

3. Use comparisons

Parenting is like
being in grade school, and the teacher asks the whole class:
What are you afraid of?
The first kid says: A world without love.
The next one says: poisonous snakes, and also lava.
I can't manage an answer because they both have good points.

4.   Use a character

My mother-in-law made each one of her children write:
A fart is not a joke
in longhand, at least a hundred times if not more—
accounts vary between brothers and in the telling.
So here's my husband, trying to explain to the kid
we are actually very awesome parents
because we tread the middle ground
appreciating the uncomplicated joy of the low brow...
But seriously, dude, you have to know: you can't do that in class
or when we have company
or when we're out in public
or at a restaurant
or at the library
or in front of grandma—definitely not in front of grandma.
There's a time and place for everything.
and my son nods seriously and sagely
as he lets one rip.
Glorious crescendo, great resonant tone, precocious control.
He keeps a perfectly straight face as he intones:
I think I timed that right.

5.   Callback to an earlier moment

Look, what he actually said was
I like you.

Then he fell asleep in my arms.
But I didn't know that in the moment
so why should you?

Both lessons are stones I hold in my pocket
turning them over and over until
these heavy little things are
smooth and warm and almost indistinguishable.

Ice In The Desert

before, when it was just desert and tents
no radio, electric lights, butane cook stoves

I wonder if the world felt vast
when we could not pinpoint each other on a map

we knew how to make ice, before we invented
written language, the timeline an open question

of priorities, elemental needs unfolding in
purposeful order—what can we learn from this

or coincidence, the lucky discovery in which we recognize
desire before we understand what we've done

I file this fact with cross references:
revelatory history, human ingenuity, survival skills, miracle

our ancestors, too ancient to trace through trees
we bind ourselves with DNA swabs and family legend

those nomads made long, shallow pools lined with stone
filled them with water in the early evening hours, then

returned before first light to collect
the ice, then stored in hollow domes over deep holes

as you unpack the implications of science deformed
by imagination let me whisper the poetics of the process

water laid out throws heat in the form of light
on cloudless desert night, all space is laid bare above us

our atmosphere cannot hold on to what radiates
and a window opens to the universe

light, which is heat, which is energy, sent to and through the sky
giving more, giving up, cooling faster than

the world around it, island of change, of
metamorphic discovery. We are the ice, born

too early in time to be understood, loved nonetheless, we
are the stars, receiving more than we return.

Nakedness III

The parents are very confused because they can't find the child who is bleeding, but someone must be hurt and why is one naked and running away into the backyard and no one is making sense. Who's hurt? In their own time, each adult comes to the conclusion: we will laugh about this later. Right now, everyone focuses very hard on showing how serious this is.

Spring Cleaning

I can't say I know why today is the day
I decided to clean the refrigerator.

Do not think less of me when I tell you
how bad it was. I feel, deep down

black mold is not something that just happens to anyone -
it must have been brought on by some inadequacy,

a moral failing, above and beyond refusal
to domesticate properly, to clean house daily

the meditation and obligation of the wife.
There's no surprise here in the state of things.

The infestation has been growing. Maybe the scope
is greater than I'd imagined or wanted to see.

Maybe the shame so deeply programmed is unexpected
even as I refuse delivery. The cleaning is

cathartic. Today I am merciless with the condiments,
the barely perishables, maraschino cherries and garlic pickle

still good but purged, the green tomato relish
bought last summer on the road trip south

where we passed by my relatives but said nothing,
like the old days when no one needed to know

where in the world you might be
no blinking light on the map of a GPS, tracked, known.

I prefer to move through this world invisible and
unobligated. Why should blood be thicker than

pain, openly acknowledged and traced to its source?
Keep only the hunger for piccalilli. It won't keep long

but it can be kept in the back of the second shelf
until today, when I come to terms, come to my senses.

I squeal, my fingers slipping into the onion
that looked solid but has quietly liquefied in a drawer.

I have not purged my family from the flickering feeds
that scroll by in memes that look just like real life if you squint

or become exhausted enough to let things blur, the weight
of pixels and molecules, history and small lives and teetering

between what mattered and what matters;
with everything salvageable on the counter

I took the shelving apart
bleached the glass and scrubbed.

Paper towels, real towels, an old toothbrush
everything open, stripped, scoured.

Look—I knew, OK, that things were out of hand.
garlic and rancid dill and earthen must—

fragile things gone off even as I told myself
the fixing was more trouble than soldiering on

maybe it would resolve on its own.
We were so busy, all winter. Fall before that.

What then, is the takeaway? That hope
is achievable time after time with enough elbow grease

and willingness to finally throw away remnants
of all the things that will go uneaten, even if they

are not spoiled yet? Or is it bleak, no matter
what I've done today, I know I can't defeat

the mold. It will return, re-colonize over time
the internal conditions always perfect for its bloom.

There is nothing, nothing to do but
fight it back regularly or in giant bursts

of inspiration and unlikely motivation.

Raccoon Attack

This morning all business of busy-ness, the work of getting stuff done, fine mist of nonspecific out-of-sorts slicks everything, clings to your lungs. Muscle through never ending list of to-do's, resorting to things that can be crossed off free of inspiration: move forward, heave and lurch and labor: forward, onward, onward, until there's a groove to fall into. Sit for coffee at last, stare through the email, let your gaze wander.

Through the sliding glass door I finally see: *last night things happened.*

The screen door ripped, something has come into the porch. Scrabbling hands gone through the trashcan that was tucked into a corner, upended everything. The garbage I'd forgotten about, picked over, spread all over the slate tiles I just swept I just swept I just swept over the weekend thinking it would be nice to feel beautiful and tidy is close.

The world chips through and floods me—most snakes will vomit when faced with stress and I fixate with nausea on how very unaware I have been, blind to new chaos, impervious to probabilistic atomic decay.

                         I mean, it's been like this, obviously.

                         It's already done and unavoidable, but I spent the morning blithe, saturated in the tasks of an outdated world like the tree that fell in last year's ice storm. Broken, tied to the taproot by a thread, it bloomed where it lay, didn't finish dying until almost July. Now is the joyless singing of the stomach on comfortless roller coaster, spiraling, rising, plummeting.

The raccoons have realized that my screen is as fragile as a social convention and I do not know what to do now.

Americana

The first weekend of June we
are reckless with our time, out in the still
sunbright evening because we are ready

for summer to shift our lives in earnest
weightless languor and easier breathing
no matter how little changes in the details.

My son, my husband, and I pick up and go together
to the ball field where the high school baseball team drills—
white man-sized changelings dancing

against Parrish blue sky and golden clouds
the woods greener than I can understand, behind them.
We play too. I sit in the grass and watch,

which is an all consuming endeavor.
Thunk of the ball hitting the bat and
soundless scurry of feet until soft pat:

glove finding purpose. I see, I hear,
the senses blend until I am seeing the crack of each hit
hearing the smile of my son, tasting the joy in his

dive to the grass. Flying through
the single straight line I open with my attention:
a swallow, a butterfly, a clump of floral fluff.

I would fix this alignment this great conjunction in
something more visual than song, it steals
breath, this moment becomes amber,

I am stuck in liquid time turned stone.
The bird is fast, wings sharp as bullets,
its hollow bones aimed with precision

as it eats its own weight at the boundary
of earth and sky, also, it flies for joy
we're told. And the butterfly

seems aimless, but look how the light
becomes more golden on its flank.
Oh, what it has gone through to be here

in this form, and know how far it will travel
to mass before falling like tickertape
carpet on the forest floor. The plumose cluster

tangle of threads built to fly seeds
far from their start, catch the breeze and
sail smooth as if it were easy. Americana.

If only you could see through my eyes.
This is mine, mine, the small puddle and the
ugly complicated ideal that snakes

forward and backward in time, unhinging
its jaw to swallow whatever it's crushed.
I tear as my child laughs;

he has caught the ball, pop fly to right center
and we quit while we're ahead,
holding hands on the way back to the car.

Revelation, In One Act

The curtain rises like eyes being pried open, like a down comforter being pulled from you, all the heat you could possibly make falling out of the opening where the light spills in.

Child: MOM! MOM! Quick I need you right now!

All lights up full.

Anticipation catches like a breath.

Child: Look—the clock is 5, 4, 3.

Long pause.

Child: That's so cool, right?

The end.

Ok, here is why theater is better than movies: because you are trapped in the same room with no escape. But still the curtain closes on a scene. This is how you know it is better and worse and a different thing entirely from and maybe truer to life. Sometimes the stage manager comes through and you did not hear exactly but you find yourself calling out: thank you, five minutes. Reality is something you imagined might pull you apart, but sometimes it tangles around you in a squeeze. Do not forget to breathe.

Finalists in the One Word Play Contest

Yes.
No.
But.
Breathe.
Regret.
This.
Sweetheart.
Sing.
Embrace.
Why?
Rend.
Nail.
Unspoken.
Never.
Pregnant.
I…
Fading.
Shuffle.
Goodbye.
… … … …OK.
Once.
Go.
Leap.
Stride.
Boom.
HA!
Want.
Now?
Gnawing.
Now.
Bend.
Need.
Tomorrow.
Fuck.
Bleeding.
Stop.

With a Heavy Heart I Must Tell You

They say heavy is the head
(with responsibility) as if my head
did not float; whatever mad science

machinery of tubing and steam
meant to condense thought to syrup
fragrant hints into flavor, thicker—

heavy, viscous, true
mine has shattered into infinite glass
glitter too granular to call shards

these pieces mist irreparable, my mind
fogs light and lighted, less dense
than the air around me, than time,

than each breath that perches on my chest
like a rock trial, judgement of pressing
oh, I remember, clouds are

heavy, heavier than buses yet
they soar, this is magic, physics, magic and I
am glowing dull as embers with awe

heavy is the head is the heart is the
inner voice that pushes you around but
is silent silenced in the middle of the night

when worries burrow in, the plump kind
that slowly nibble gangrenous edges alongside
the swifter kind that head straight

for the meat of the heart.

Nakedness IV

The next day, the mother of the boy is drinking her coffee and telling the story to a friend with her own boys who lives far away and does not know the other players so she convinces herself it is not a betrayal to laugh about it, to make sense aloud at a safe distance. Especially she admits the elation: it was not my child who triggered the mess, who transgressed, who showed everyone everything. She is happy in the way of the humble lucky, knowing full well there was nothing particular she did or did not do as a parent to prevent his exposure, or hers, the human frailty of is all, the inexplicable moments of childhood when it all barrels forward at full speed and the choices we make are as graceful as a newborn giraffe. We are falling down in every direction.

Some Facts for This Moment

1.
Not only is man far from the only animal to use tools, some birds have even been observed making and using prosthetics—mostly artificial legs, after losing them to predators, sometimes in botched attempts to save a nest and fledglings, but one ostrich was observed replacing its wing even though it could obviously not fly.

2.
Pluto is highly unstable and will likely fracture itself in a geologically near future. This, of course, is one of the main reasons its planetary status was revoked, even though scientists deny any such bias based on unpredictability and fragility.

3.
Despite popular mythology having Joan of Arc cropping her hair short like a boy's, she actually invented the French twist, later popularized by Grace Kelly, whose marriage into the Monaco monarchy gained her ownership of the castle where Joan's mortal remains were interred. Some of them.

4.
Squirrels only hide nuts in caches of odd numbers. They feel great about their prospects for the winter, but many will die before spring.

5.
One of the great pyramids is sinking, slowly but surely, and it is illegal under Egyptian law to photograph the now obvious difference. Older images hid the discrepancy with perspective and unusual angles.

6.
In upper Scandinavia, where the sun sets for a fortnight over solstice, reindeer faint at first light each year. One myth casts this as relief that the sun has returned, but scientific study finds that the endocrinology is identical to that of the beasts' reaction to very large bears and repeated sonic booms, so they are certain it is pure fear.

7.
Debussy was colorblind. Ironically, he tends to be a favorite of synesthetes, particularly his nocturnes. I have been known to cry, seeing what he fumbled into.

NOTE: "Some Facts for This Moment" was written in response to our post-truth times. To dispel any confusion, none of the listed are (facts).

Whose Side Are You On?

If you grow rhubarb in the dark
it will be sweeter;
the strings of their stalks will

soften, bend, the whole
becoming red,
redder, flushing bright

in comparison
to ordinary farming
in the sunlight, things planted once.

No, to make this violent abortifacient
tame, you let it grow two years
then move it to total darkness

where the roots tangle so closely
you can hear them squeaking
as they grow past each other,

shoving through dirt -
the stretch of their stalks will
pop, crack, creak, the rub

of growth and seeking
for what we have hidden:
the light, of course, I mean

the light.

My Grief Has Not Faded, She Has Split Herself In Two
    for BG

One has softened, grown warm and round.
When we see each other, that grief greets me
with a hug, mutual embrace, neither clinging.

We place ourselves in the other's arm to understand weight.
We are more or and less heavy at any given moment,
me and my grief, like a pebble in a pocket who does not know

whether it has been ferried to sea level or space.
Gravity must be relearned in each moment.
This grief whispers golden light and thick honey

and I swallow, what is sometimes sweetness and sometimes
a painful wad that stretches my throat, catches in the dent
above my collarbone. We are almost friends. The other is undulled,

a trickster with razor blades who hungers for the raw
and must be fed dearly, like a newborn learning to latch
cannot be fully unloved for the pain, for her fulfilled id.

This grief hunts my gaze and trespasses
at the edge of my vision, in a crowd, and
for that half moment I forget

the soul that I think is that shape is gone.
Still gone. Sometimes she hovers invisible
to plant a scent, to solder this live wire

direct electric bypass to the void I hold
Heart and breath arrested. In her presence I am always unhealed.
She always catches me by surprise.

Nakedness V

Days later the neighbor is telling an unrelated story about her hairdresser, who just got back from France where she accidentally wandered onto a nude beach. She was uncomfortable being in a bikini with everyone else naked, but she was uncomfortable too with the idea of walking around naked, even if no one knew her or cared or any of that. But what she really couldn't process was the sight of all the families, moms, dads, lots of kids, all happily playing, seeing everything, everything, everything. You can't unsee it, you know? Even if you're brought up to think it's natural and normal, if you grow up and don't want to know what your mom looks like naked, too bad, it's there in your memory, and your dad too. Everything.

Irony

To bury something
effectively
you must
dig deep—
which means a friend,
looking in
on this very scene
looking at
you
cannot be sure
this is a different act
from unburying

secrets long
locked safely
in the dirt
beneath us.

Haunting

No, ghosts are what you dig up, solid and lumpy and grown
to their own design. Whisper incomplete secrets into the opening
of a burl and wait—until the chafing from the bark has healed
on your cheek and at least three rains. Search where you do not expect
anything to be underground—here, it's all connected
the way we grasp a single root and shudder as it twitches and swells.
Ghosts lie there like potatoes, and you must unearth them without tools
save your own hands. Left long enough, the heart wrinkles and feeds
sprouts pushing into the air to become perennial haunts
bearing elderflowers, and if pollinated, elderberries
the juice wine-dark and collected, reduced by the careless
into cyanide. The philosophy professor sickened herself
in just such a manner, as though she should have known better.
We only say that because she is well versed in the classics
and has collected prestige to her nest like magpies stealing
tin bits from the shoulder of the highway, twisted scraps but
shiny, precious and sharp and prophetic, really, but only
if you know how to scry. I keep my ghosts in the pockets
of winter coats, with a ten dollar bill and loose change that
I will find after a summer in the closet and think I am
lucky and rich and the additional weight will not worry me
tugging at my profile like everyday grief. In the absence
of an answer, I'll keep carrying it around.

The Sun Is Just Another Every Day Grief

The sun is just another every day grief that
hangs heavy in the sky, unimaginable
Even when it burns in plain sight.

We tell ourselves it cannot rip the velvet
Where it dangles, pulls its weight towards us
On just the one precarious hook.

Here For It All
    For JAM

We are at a picnic, the week after we have both gone to funerals,
fought lice, scrambled to make lunch with just the heel of the loaf, nothing

left but the crunchy kind of peanut butter. I am mostly not crying as we watch
our children running barefoot. It's too much, too much, I say. I'm in my head

and drowning. Who can fight existentialism and do dishes at the same time?
She says, well, we have come to the place in our lives where life and death are

messy and present—the jagged edges of absences sitting next to us,
their shape and gravity recognized, heavy enough to pull tides of salt sea

in our bodies. We are at the place in our lives where our ghosts have names
our fears are hard like the ground at the end of a fall, soft like flesh

with its owner gone missing in the night, as we caress what is left, begging
our memory to trap this sensation, this touch, this goodbye as faithfully as
    our first

kiss. But our body will not, cannot, remember this, so we will let
our muscles imagine all we need our grief to be: emptiness in infinite
    particulars.

We have come to the place where we know a hole is a thing all its own.
We hold what it is and not what we've lost. We try to hold each other but

our fears—now hard, now soft—scuttle over our feet each night when we
    should
be sleeping. Superstition laughs and says someone, someone has just walked
    over

your grave. Oh, momma, oh child. At the end of the singing, we light sparklers
and hold them to the sky. That night my son asks for dessert and I give it to
    him

because he is here and hungry and can eat and I can hold him
an extra ten minutes before bed as the ice cream melts over us.

Thanks

With gratitude for the friendship, mentorship, and tremendous gift of knowing Jon Woocher, Bill Goldman, and Jeanne Austin McIntosh. Special thanks to early readers Lauren Horne and Stacy Rachels, to the best book club in Greater New Haven for encouragement and support in all endeavors, the divas of Lanman Wright and beyond, the cul de sac and its kids whose naked shenanigans are preserved herein. Deep continuing thanks to Sherre Vernon, whose compatible heart and masterful craft have helped me grow, to my cosmic twin the Other Shana, and above all to my loving husband and son.

Shana Ross is a writer, mother, occasional muse, sometime wallflower, middle aged ambivert with a BA and MBA from Yale University. She pays her bills as a consultant and leadership expert, bringing aspects of the arts (and quite a few poems) into the lives of business leaders and students around the world. Since resuming her writing career in 2018, she has accumulated a number of publication credits, both poetry and speculative fiction.

Shana lives with her husband, son, and three cats in Edmonton, Alberta. Since 2020, her household also includes a rather demanding sourdough starter. She periodically takes up running, if only to catch up on the podcasts she's missed. She prefers long walks with friends.

Dedicated to a growth mindset, Shana is delighted to be an emerging writer with a few extra years of life experience to feed her work. Heavy Little Things, a meditation on grief and parenthood, is her first collection.

www.ingramcontent.com/pod-product-compliance
Lightning Source LLC
LaVergne TN
LVHW041601070426
835507LV00011B/1230